Pirates and Privateers

Jeremy Pascall

Sampson Low

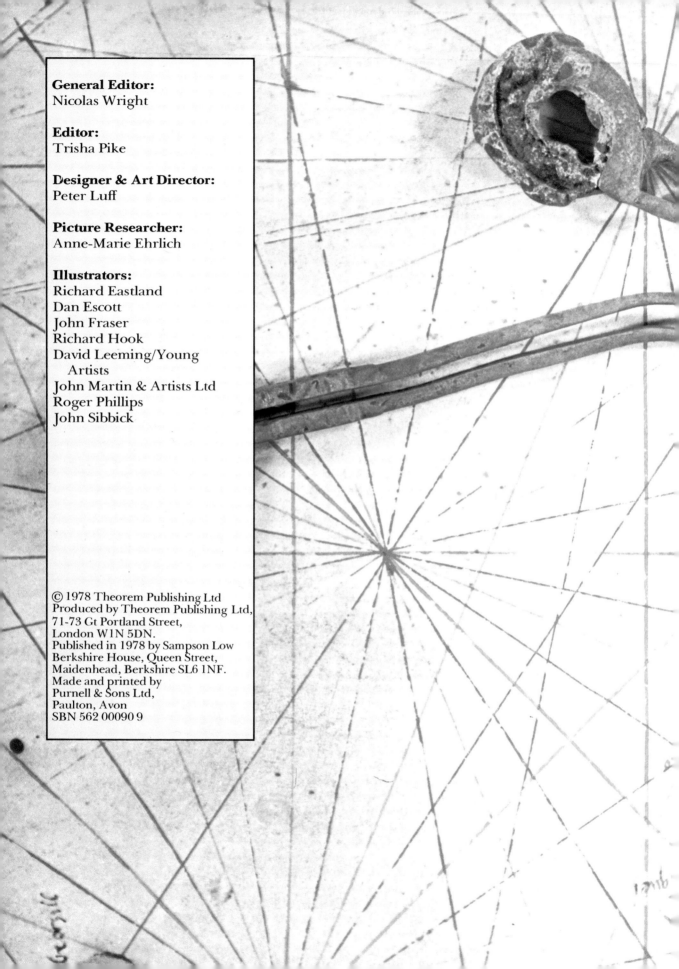

General Editor:
Nicolas Wright

Editor:
Trisha Pike

Designer & Art Director:
Peter Luff

Picture Researcher:
Anne-Marie Ehrlich

Illustrators:
Richard Eastland
Dan Escott
John Fraser
Richard Hook
David Leeming/Young
   Artists
John Martin & Artists Ltd
Roger Phillips
John Sibbick

Produced by Theorem Publishing Ltd,
71-73 Gt Portland Street,
London W1N 5DN.
Published in 1978 by Sampson Low
Berkshire House, Queen Street,
Maidenhead, Berkshire SL6 1NF.
Made and printed by
Purnell & Sons Ltd,
Paulton, Avon
SBN 562 00090 9

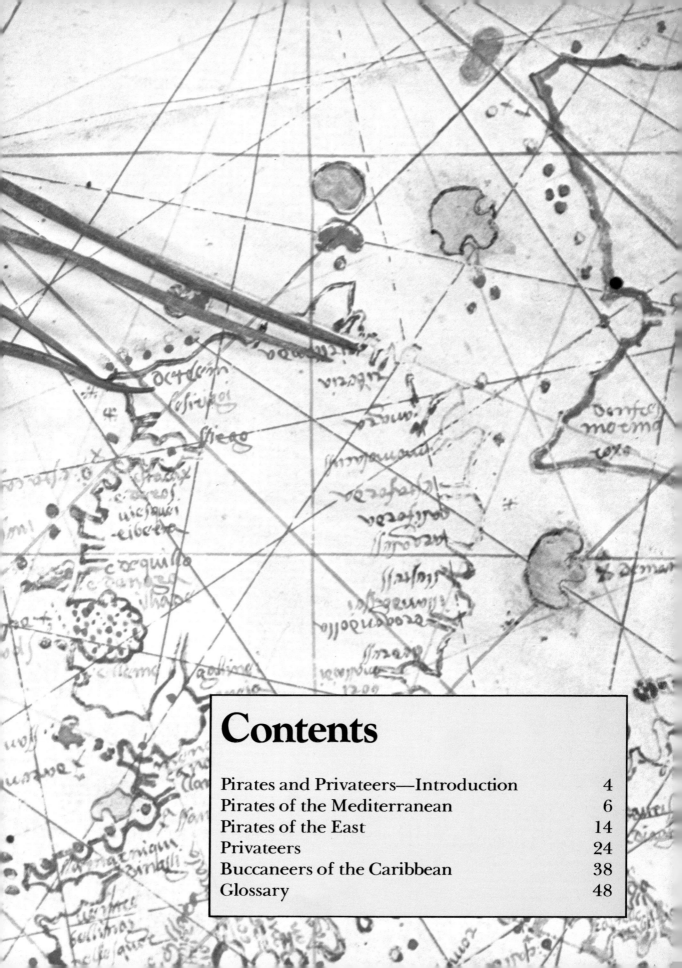

Contents

Pirates and Privateers—Introduction 4
Pirates of the Mediterranean 6
Pirates of the East 14
Privateers 24
Buccaneers of the Caribbean 38
Glossary 48

Pirates and Privateers

Life at sea was hard and dangerous for the crews of merchant ships during the 17th and 18th centuries. Food was poor and scanty, conditions harsh and unhealthy and there was the constant threat of storms and gales. There was, however, an extra hazard to shipping—piracy. Crews of ruthless pirates roved the seas striking at any well-laden merchant ship they came upon. Their skill and seamanship enabled them to escape pursuit by warships, and the prices on the heads of pirate crews ensured they fought to the death to escape capture.

On the whole pirates worked for themselves, but some were officially authorized by their countries to carry out acts of piracy. These men were known as privateers. This sometimes happened in times of war, when captains of vessels would be issued with Letters of Marque, which were commissions to attack and rob enemy galleons. Treasure captured from these galleons was shared between the monarch and the privateers, and was regarded as spoils of war.

There was very little difference, therefore, between piracy and privateering. English privateers were considered to be pirates by Spain, and vice versa. In fact, captured pirates often claimed that they were privateers working in the service of their country. Also, some English privateers, who were legally allowed to attack only Spanish ships, could not resist the occasional temptation to attack a French merchantman. This was, however, considered an act of piracy, by the English authorities as well as the French.

In spite of the hazards, hundreds of men joined pirate crews, lured by the thrill of adventure and the promise of riches. A great many pirates were originally sailors who had served in the navies and merchant fleets of their homeland, deserting because of dreadful conditions, poor pay and brutal discipline.

Some pirates, like the Frenchman Ravenaux de Luson, were the black sheep of noble families and abandoned their responsibilities for a life of danger and excitement. Others, however, were just ruthless villains: Blackbeard, Calico Jack, Henry Morgan, Captain Kidd, and the dreaded L'Olonnois—known simply as 'The Torturer'. Many started as privateers, but at the end of the war which had allowed them to plunder legally, they turned to piracy. Piracy was at its height from 1700 to 1800, but had declined by the time Nelson had routed the French at Trafalgar in 1805. In the east, particularly in the China Sea and around the islands of Indonesia, piracy continued well into the 20th century; in 1962 there were approximately 40 attacks made on vessels sailing off the coast of North Borneo.

Above: The 16th-century English privateers considered it their duty to attack Spanish merchant ships. These operations yielded fabulous treasures such as coins and gold jewellery.

Right: When French privateers on board *Jeune Richard* attacked *The Winsor Castle* they found that their vessel was no match for the English mail packet.

Pirates of the Mediterranean

For as long as ships have carried valuable cargoes there have been pirates prepared to raid them. The word 'pirate' indicates the age of the activity. It comes from the classical Greek word *peirates* and the Latin *pirata*. Greece and Rome were the centres of the ancient civilized world. Both had coastlines along the Mediterranean Sea whose waters became the most important maritime trade routes. They also became major hunting-grounds for pirates.

The Philistines, who came from an area that is now the modern state of Israel, cruised the Aegean Sea between Greece and Turkey attacking merchant ships. In the twelfth century B.C. they attacked the Egyptian fleet of Pharaoh Rameses III, but this great sea battle ended in total defeat for the Philistines. Similarly, the Phoenicians spread out of what is now the Syrian coast to plunder shipping and sell the crews into slavery. The Greeks were skilled sailors and long before their civilization flowered considered acts of piracy as part of normal trading. Indeed, the Greek historian Herodotus was

Above: Piracy on the high seas was commonplace among the ancient Greeks. One such incident is illustrated on this cup and shows a merchant vessel pursued by a warship. Left: The Mediterranean was the most important trade route of the ancient world.

so surprised that there were seafaring merchants who were *not* pirates, he made special mention of them in his writings.

To the Romans, the pirates who infested the Mediterranean were a considerable menace. At the height of the empire, wealth and supplies poured into Rome from its widely-scattered lands. The most vital cargoes carried wheat from Egypt, and grain ships were attacked regularly by the marauders. In 78 B.C. the young Julius Caesar was captured and held to ransom when pirates from Asia Minor (modern Turkey) boarded the ship on which he was travelling. When he was eventually released in exchange for a large sum of money, he assembled four galleys manned by 500 soldiers and led a successful assault on the pirates' garrison.

Eleven years later, in 67 B.C., pirates were so powerful that they virtually controlled the eastern Mediterranean and even launched raids on Rome's main seaport, Ostia. Alarmed by these attacks, the Roman authorities ordered their most successful military commander, Pompey (Gnaeus Pompeius), to rid the sea of them once and for all. He mustered a fleet of 500 ships and swept through the Mediterranean from west to east. In as little as 40 days of fighting, including a fierce struggle in the pirate fortresses along Asia Minor's rugged coast, Pompey succeeded in subduing them. The pirates' grip was broken and although some continued their activities on a small scale, the Mediterranean was not seriously threatened again until after the collapse of the Roman Empire.

Sleek, fast pirate vessels from Asia Minor (modern Turkey) bear down on a Roman merchantman in which the young Julius Caesar travels.

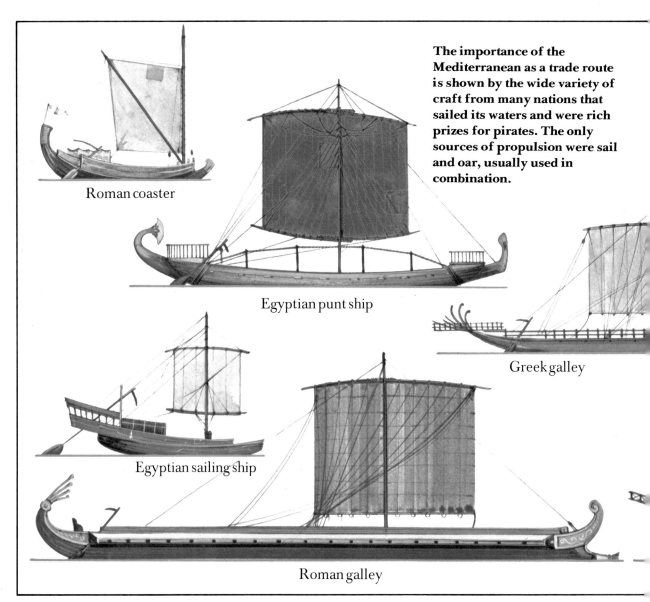

The importance of the Mediterranean as a trade route is shown by the wide variety of craft from many nations that sailed its waters and were rich prizes for pirates. The only sources of propulsion were sail and oar, usually used in combination.

Roman coaster

Egyptian punt ship

Greek galley

Egyptian sailing ship

Roman galley

The collapse of the Roman Empire was a slow process. It was attacked from the north by fierce warrior tribes which swept down from north-east Germany through Gaul (France), Spain and North Africa and sacked Rome in A.D. 455.

Conquest of the Mediterranean, the stronghold of Christendom, was also the primary aim of the Moors. They came from Morocco and the Barbary Coast, the long Mediterranean sea-line that stretched from Algiers in the west, through Tunis to Tripoli in the east (these are approximately the modern states of Algeria, Tunisia and Libya). The Moors fought a holy crusade to carry the Moslem (or Islamic) faith into the heartland of hated Christianity.

To the Moors, as well as the great seafarers of Venice, piracy was a way of life. For the Moors, and the Ottoman Turks who followed them into conquest of the

Right: Admiral Kheireddin Barbarossa's pirate fleet.

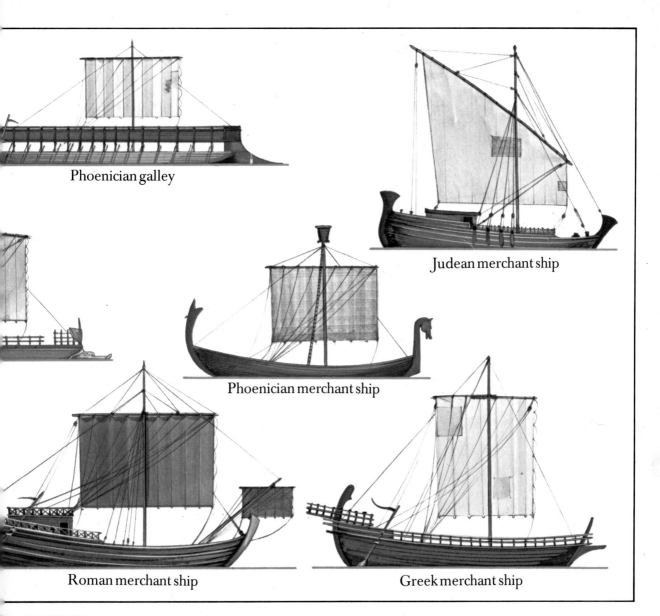

Phoenician galley

Judean merchant ship

Phoenician merchant ship

Roman merchant ship

Greek merchant ship

Mediterranean, piracy was simply a part of their fight against Christianity. By the 16th century the Ottoman Empire controlled the Barbary Coast, the rest of North Africa to the east of it, the coastline of the Middle East (modern Israel, Lebanon and Syria) and all of Anatolia (modern Turkey). However, almost all the rest of the north European Mediterranean coast (from Greece in the east to Spain in the west) was Christian. Each controlled only half the Mediterranean and yet both needed the whole of its waters for vital trading routes. Although most of the great land battles between Moslems and Christians were over, the Holy War still continued at sea, carried on by the aggressive actions of the corsairs. These were privateers licensed to attack enemy shipping. The Moslem corsairs operated out of the Barbary Coast and were consequently known as Barbary corsairs; their Christian counterparts centred around Malta, right in the middle of the Mediterranean. They were mostly acting under

9

licence from the Grand Master of the Order of the Knights of St John and were known as Maltese corsairs.

At first they both acted as Christian and Moslem navies, preying upon the shipping of each other and dividing their spoils with their masters. Malta generally received one-tenth of the prize and Barbary one-eighth. Later, individual adventurers were commissioned and conducted themselves like the better-known privateers, such as John Hawkins and Francis Drake, who attacked the galleons of Spain.

The Barbary corsairs sailed into the Christian waters of the eastern Mediterranean, seeking out ships and attacking coastal towns. The Maltese corsairs carried out the same acts in the Moslem part of the sea. Occasionally, fleets of opposing corsairs engaged in spectacular sea battles and the capture of an enemy ship and its crew was considered a great prize.

Unlike the privateers and pirates that followed, the main plunder of the corsairs was not treasure or valuable cargo, but ships and men who were sold into slavery. Many ended their days as galley slaves, for until the end of the 17th century oar-power was the most common propulsion for ships of the Mediterranean fleets.

The Barbary corsairs soon gained a reputation as wild and cruel people. They were said to appear out of the mist in their galleys, firing cannon mounted in the bows. They also used smaller swivel-guns to kill and injure the crew of the enemy ship. Once the corsair vessel had come alongside its target hordes of terrifying brigands swarmed onto the decks. The corsairs were easily identified in their eastern pantaloons, brightly-coloured turbans, and curved scimitars. Some also wore richly-adorned breast armour. Many legends grew up around these bold and ruthless men. Most notable were the brothers Arouj and Kheireddin. Because of their flaming red beards, the brothers were known throughout the Mediterranean as the Barbarossas, after the twelfth-century Holy Roman Emperor Frederick Barbarossa. Although both these wily brigands terrorized the seas, the elder brother Arouj was the more reckless of the two. After a brief but bloody battle in 1504 he captured an enemy galley belonging to the Pope, despite its greater size and superior manpower. Later that day the galley's sister ship appeared. Arouj ordered his men to conceal themselves, while the Christian slaves were forced to man the deck and pretend to be sailors. The two ships sailed close together; the unsuspecting crew of the Pope's galley were showered with a deadly hail of arrows, and the corsair boarding party soon overpowered the remaining crew.

Arouj's plundering was so effective that the Spanish launched a campaign against corsair strongholds in Barbary. During one of the battles that followed, Arouj lost an arm. This made him a more determined corsair and he joined forces with the Algerians to rout the Spaniards from the coast. However, he had greater ambitions and after defeating the Spanish he gained control of Algiers by murdering the Emir. His reign was so tyrannical that both Algiers and Spain turned against him, combining to drive him out.

Arouj and Kheireddin Barbarossa were the scourge of Christian seafarers in the Mediterranean. The most feared of all the Barbary corsairs, they gained the nickname Barbarossa which translates as 'red beard'. Arouj was merely a villain but his younger brother was an intelligent and respected leader whose military cunning gained him the rank of admiral.

The constant battles between Christian and Moslem corsairs in the Mediterranean resulted in a Holy War. Admiral Kheireddin Barbarossa was a wily tactician, and his success was the result of intelligent and careful planning. The map (inset) was drawn by his naval architect and shows the French port of Marseilles. When Barbary corsairs struck (as depicted in the painting below, dated 1661, by Cornelius Vroom) the fight was usually bloody and the tortures inflicted were terrible and merciless.

Kheireddin shared his brother Arouj's daring but was a better tactician and diplomat. He offered his services to the Sultan of Turkey in an assault against the Spanish fort on the island off Algiers called Peñon d'Alger. Two weeks of bombardment left the garrison in ruins and from the rubble Kheireddin built a massive breakwater, using slave labour, to protect the port from any further attacks.

Kheireddin attacked ships within the Mediterranean, and he also sailed through the Straits of Gibraltar and into the Atlantic Ocean. Here he lay in wait for Spanish galleons laden with cargo from the Americas. He continued a successful career of piracy for many years and, unlike so many of his 'profession', lived to a great age.

The Christian counterparts of the Barbary corsairs were the corsairs from Malta. The Moslem Barbary corsairs had a grim reputation, but the Christians were no less greedy or bloodthirsty.

The men who made up the crews of the Christian Maltese corsairs were mainly French, Italian, Greek, Corsican, Sicilian and, of course, Maltese. They were frequently professional seaman who turned from employment in the navies and merchant fleets of the nations of the Mediterranean to the more profitable trade of licensed piracy.

Life aboard a corsair vessel was much easier than in the conventional navy or merchant marine. Discipline tended to be fairly relaxed as each man was regarded as an equal partner in a risky venture. The officers were paid not so much for their rank, as for their skill at the crafts of seamanship. Indeed, many corsairs were not experienced sailors at all but soldiers who fought at sea rather than on land.

Right: The Chinese pirates were a major threat to British trade in the Far East. The navy resolved to sweep these brigands from the sea and launched a series of attacks against their strongholds. They directed their actions against the pirates' shore bases and often had to fight off assaults from junks at the same time.
Below: This painting of Canton in 1810 shows the impact made on China by British and Western trading nations.

Pirates of the East

Although the best-known pirates were those of the Caribbean, the most pirate-infested seas were undoubtedly those of the east. The waters of the Indian Ocean and the China Sea were plagued by them. They hid in the inlets and bays of the hundreds of islands running from Malaysia, through Sumatra, Borneo to the Philippines. In the 19th century the great British pirate hunter Admiral the Hon. Henry Keppel said: 'As surely as spiders abound where there are nooks and crannies, so have pirates sprung up wherever there is a nest of islands offering creeks and shallows, headlands, rocks and reefs—facilities in short for lurking, for attack, for escape.'

From the time of Christ, pirates had cruised the eastern seas, preying on merchant ships carrying valuable cargoes of precious metals, gems, silks and spices between Arabia, India, the Indonesian chain and China. Many small coastal states grew up and made war upon their neighbours. Their navies were usually fleets of small, swift, oar-powered vessels and were no better than licensed pirates.

14

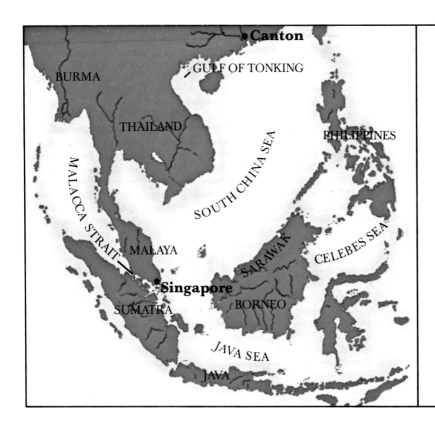

Above: Britain's most important possession was Singapore (at the tip of Malaya) which became a bustling modern port.
Left: The thousands of islands in the South China Sea offered perfect hiding places for the pirates who terrorized this vast area.

Until the end of the 15th century piracy in the east was largely an internal affair, the victims being Chinese junks and vessels from India, Thailand and other eastern states. However, in 1497, the Portuguese navigator, Vasco da Gama rounded the Cape of Good Hope at the southernmost tip of Africa and sailed into the Indian Ocean. Henceforth the European nations had access to the vast treasures of India, Arabia and even China. The English, French, Spanish, Portuguese and Dutch soon started trading with, and then colonizing, the countries east of Africa. As more and more European merchantmen sailed round the Cape, piracy in these seas increased alarmingly. By the 19th century, Britain ruled India and trade with China had created the vital seafaring market of Singapore. At this time the menace from pirates was so great that decisive action had to be taken. Piratical activity centred around three areas—the Malay peninsula (especially the Malacca Strait between Sumatra and Malaya), Borneo and the trade routes of the China Sea.

The most important British possession in Malaya was Singapore. Stamford Raffles, the British founder of Singapore, had established the port in 1819 as a 'halfway house' for trade. Chinese junks filled the harbour and off-loaded their cargoes of silk, tea and other valuables. These they exchanged for English textiles which they carried back to their own merchants. Malaysian craft traded their cargo of spices for British goods and all the exotic eastern commodities were loaded into huge British merchantmen to be carried back on the long voyage round the Horn to England. The region had always been a pirate stronghold but the massive

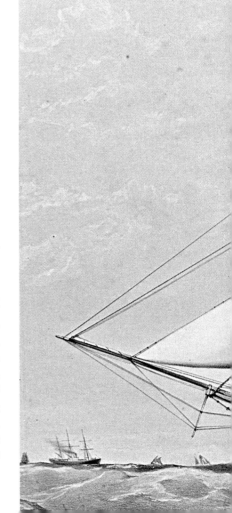

increase in trade that Singapore stimulated, encouraged more and more pirates. They flocked from the coasts of Sumatra and Malaya, attracted by rich and easy pickings. For 16 years the pirates had the upper hand because, despite continual appeals from traders and merchants, the authorities refused to consider them a serious threat.

The Malays were expert sailors; they put to sea in long, swift perahu propelled by about 100 galley slaves and carrying as many as 150 warriors armed with muskets, swords and spears. The perahu carried a large cannon in the bows and a number of swivel-mounted guns along its length. This armament, plus the war-loving nature of the crews made them formidable opponents; they swooped down on their victims in convoy, blasted cannonfire into their target and waited for an opportunity to manoeuvre close and swarm aboard.

Before 1835, actions against the pirates were infrequent and unsuccessful. Britain's naval power suffered great humiliation when an East India Company gunboat was forced to flee in the face of a flotilla of 20 marauding perahu. After this, the indignation of the merchants whose cargoes were being ransacked was so loud that their complaints could no longer be ignored.

In 1835, a fleet of six vessels, including the 28-gun *Andromache*, were assembled with the intention of subduing

Above: Stamford Raffles, who established Singapore in 1819.

Below: Fast clippers carried trade goods around the world, in spite of the hazards of plying pirate-infested seas.

piracy. Knowing that warships would simply scare the pirates off and send them scuttling to their bases, the commander, Captain H. D. Chads, disguised his ships as merchantmen to fool the pirates. *Andromache* was camouflaged as an Arab trading ship and *Wolf* as a dealer in wild animals, complete with monkeys, bears and a panther. So convincing were these ploys that many pirates fell for the trick and were destroyed.

The fleet was also instructed to launch assaults on the pirates' land-based headquarters. Chad's primary target was the important pirate market of Gallang, an illegal equivalent of Singapore where pirates could trade their plunder, and restock their boats with food and ammunition. The British fleet sailed in with guns blazing and routed the pirates.

This action effectively broke the spirit of the Malay pirates. They still raided shipping but the authorities kept up the pressure and, in 1837, introduced the first steamship ever seen in those waters. The little *Diana*, with paddles churning and smoke billowing from her funnel, was a daunting sight. However, much more important was her ability to move when there was little wind. The oar-powered Malays had frequently attacked becalmed sailing ships. If a breeze did spring up the pirates would row to safety into the wind so that the vessel could not follow. *Diana*, however, could steam in the face of the wind and outstrip the pirates' vessels. She proved very effective and by 1850 Singapore was virtually free of pirates.

Right: Swift-moving Malay perahu chase a convoy of cargo-bearing European trading vessels. However, the pirates of the east did not always have their own way and the picture inset shows two British naval ships destroying a flotilla of Chinese pirate junks.

In September 1841 an Englishman named James Brooke was installed as Rajah of Sarawak. He had been given authority over this tiny province on the island of Borneo as a gift for helping Rajah Muda Hashim in a civil war. On gaining the throne of Sarawak Brooke was determined to stamp out piracy and turned to his friend Captain the Hon. Henry Keppel, R.N., for help. He told Keppel of the two groups of pirates, the Sarebas and Sekrang, whose strongholds were fortified villages on the rivers of those names. There were also raids by the fierce Illanun from the Philippines, and the Balanini from the Sulu Islands (situated between the north-east coast of Borneo and the Philippine island of Mindanao).

Keppel was sympathetic to Brooke's enterprise and together they set out to attack the pirates' strongholds. First they decided to rid Brooke's kingdom of its native bandits and turned against the Sarebas who, as Keppel wrote, '. . . were by far the most strongly fortified.' They assembled a strange force which was headed by Keppel's ship *Dido*. It included

Brooke's vessel *Jolly Bachelor* and a flotilla of perahu crammed with more than 400 battle-hungry Dyaks, who were a people of the region.

The objectives were three pirate villages situated on the Sarebas River or its tributaries. *Dido* was too deep in draught to negotiate the river so it was moored at its mouth. The rest of the force headed upstream to the accompaniment of terrible Sarebas war cries and war parties that made rather ineffectual skirmishes from the banks. The first village, Padeh, was protected by a barrier of tree trunks sunk into the river-bed. The Dyaks in their manoeuvrable craft made short work of ripping these out and creating a passage up which the main force could sail. Marines jumped ashore to find the village had been deserted, but they destroyed it and others in the area. The Dyaks set off into the jungle to hunt down the fugitive pirates and, much to the distress of the Europeans, cut off, and collected for trophies, the heads of any they found.

The victorious fleet then sailed on to the next village, Paku. Here they found that news of their success at Padeh had gone ahead of them and the terrified pirates had abandoned the village. This too was razed to the ground and Keppel pressed on to the remaining village of Rembas.

The pirates of Rembas did not give up without a struggle. The river had been fortified with a series of stout barriers which had to be removed and Keppel learned that the riverfront of Rembas was lined with cannon. He changed tactics, landed a large force of Dyaks and ordered them to creep through the jungle to the rear of the village and attack when they heard the frontal attack of his own men. The ruse worked perfectly and soon the largest and strongest Sarebas village was captured.

Brooke and Keppel then set out against the Sekrang who, learning of the defeat of the Sarebas, had joined forces under two merciless and brutal chiefs, Sharif Sahap and his brother Mullar, and assembled large war fleets. This time Keppel's fleet was strengthened by a shallow-draught steamship, *Phlegethon,* which was ideal for work in the rivers. Keppel repeated his tactics of direct frontal assault and, despite much stronger defences than they had previously encountered, these proved equally successful. The Sekrang had a vast armoury, much of which had been captured from British ships, but they were still defeated by Keppel's determined and gallant men. Eventually, the piratical leaders of Borneo recognized Britain's superiority. Piracy was stamped out in the region and the merchant ships could ply their routes in safety.

Strong though the pirate fleets of Malaya and Borneo had been, they were small compared with those that sailed off the coastline of China. These sometimes numbered hundreds of craft. They plundered the villages lining the shore and preyed upon the rich cargoes carried to and from China. The English had developed a passion for tea and great clippers set forth laden with silver to buy it from the Chinese emperor. With such booty to be gained the activities of pirates naturally increased.

In the mid-19th century two remarkable Englishmen joined forces to stamp out piracy around Borneo. Sir James Brooke (portrayed above by Sir Francis Grant) became Rajah of Sarawak. He was given the province by a grateful Rajah Hashim of Borneo as a reward for services rendered. The other Englishman, Captain (later Admiral) the Honourable Henry Keppel, was one of the navy's most capable fighters. Together they recruited native help and set out to attack the pirates in their strongly-defended villages (left).

One of the deadliest Chinese pirates was a woman named Ching Yih Saou who took over her husband's huge fleet on his death. The Chinese navy lost 56 craft trying to defeat her!

The Chinese navy was either unable or unwilling to curb the pirates' power and by the mid-19th century it fell to the British to wage war against them. The British had created a second vital trading point, similar to Singapore, in the leased Chinese territory of Hong Kong. Therefore, it was essential that merchant ships should be able to use it unmolested.

One of the most troublesome pirate chiefs in the mid-19th century was Shap-ng-Tsai. He and his henchman Chui Ah Poo caused havoc among trading ships; they seized over 40 junks in one swoop on a port. The British set after them in earnest when Chui murdered two British officers. Commander Hay, in H.M.S. *Columbine*, joined with the steamship *Canton* to search for portions of Shap's large and scattered fleet. They found a squadron of 14 junks and gave chase; *Columbine* concentrated on the largest vessel as Hay was convinced it was commanded by a pirate captain, perhaps even Chui himself.

After a long fight, *Columbine* cornered the junk in a coastal inlet. The water was too shallow for *Columbine* to proceed so Hay ordered marines into two small boats and sent them in to attack. Fire was briskly exchanged and eventually the junk was overpowered and boarded by the marines. Hay learned from one of the captured Chinese that Chui had been in command of the squadron and had been sailing to meet his superior at Bias Bay.

Hay called for reinforcements from Hong Kong and when they arrived, carefully searched the many coves that made up the bay. Eventually he came upon a force of 26 pirate junks and went into action. The battle lasted all day during which the navy out-gunned the pirates, destroyed most of the junks

Two battles against Shap-ng-Tsai's fleet: (above) steamship *Canton* tows H.M.S. *Columbine* into action, 1849. The final engagement (left): the navy triumph in the Gulf of Tonkin, 1850.

and battered their supply depots on the shore.

Chui was not captured but reports indicated he had been seriously wounded. However, his chief, Shap-ng-Tsai, was not in Bias Bay and the hunt for him began once more. Hay was at a disadvantage as Shap knew every one of the thousands of hiding-places. Luck was, however, on Hay's side; he spotted sails in a bay and a closer look revealed 37 junks, which were part of a fleet that totalled 64 vessels. Hay's force cut off the pirates' exit and with great care, they approached.

Shap formed 26 of his biggest warships into battle order and trained about 260 guns on to his outnumbered foes. Hay pressed forward and his luck held. A rocket from a British ship scored a direct hit. The navy's superior tactics, discipline and expertise in gunnery wrought havoc. After three days of battle 58 junks were destroyed. The little British fleet had beaten a strength of more than 1,200 guns and 3,000 men, half of whom were killed. It was a notable victory and although it did not eliminate piracy from the China Sea, it ensured that never again would massive fleets plague the area.

Privateers

'Privateers,' Horatio Nelson declared, 'were no better than pirates.' This accusation would probably have been hotly contested by some of his sea-faring forerunners. The great Elizabethan sea captains John Hawkins and Francis Drake were privateers and considered heroes by their countrymen.

As already seen, a thin line of legality separated privateers from pirates. The important document that granted privateers their licence to plunder the merchant shipping of a hostile nation was the 'Letter of Marque'. This was issued by the sovereign or a senior Government official and allowed the bearer to attack and rob vessels of enemy countries without fear of being prosecuted for piracy. This policy was practised by many nations, but most energetically by the British and French, and benefited them in two ways: firstly, it harassed enemy shipping and secondly, successful privateers could help swell the crown's coffers because the booty was shared between the privateer's captain and crew and the sovereign. (The proportion the crown took was generally ten per cent, the understanding being that the privateer received no financial backing. The privateer profited on results—if no ship's treasure was captured then there was no reward or pay for the crew.)

John Hawkins was a wealthy English sea captain who made his money running slaves from Africa to sell in the Spanish colonies of the New World. He was a highly successful adventurer but in 1569 his luck seemed to run out. In the face of a mighty gale he was forced to seek shelter in the port of San Juan de Ulloa (on what is now the Mexican coast) with his three tiny, storm-battered vessels. At the same time the Spanish were expecting the arrival of a treasure fleet. Hawkins knew the Spanish suspected him of piracy and were unlikely to be friendly towards him. He was thus caught between risking his leaky ships in the gale, or being fired upon by the Spanish warships escorting the treasure fleet.

Hawkins finally decided that his best course was to try to negotiate a truce, until the gale had passed and he could set course for England. After wary talks, the Spanish eventually agreed to allow the English ships to anchor in the port. However, the Spanish commander secretly planned the capture of Hawkins and his ships and two days after the truce they launched their attack on the unsuspecting Englishmen. In the fight that followed, the largest English ship, *Jesus Of Lubeck*, was lost and many sailors were killed or captured. The rest narrowly escaped in the remaining ships *Minion* and *Judith*. No-one involved in the action ever forgot this treacherous attack. In particular, the commander of the little ship *Judith* devoted his life to seeking revenge, and became a sworn enemy of Spain. This man was John Hawkins's cousin, and his name was Francis Drake.

So destructive were Drake's forays against the

Above: Queen Elizabeth I turned a blind eye to some of the not strictly legal activities of her favourite sea captains.

Above: Sir John Hawkins was one of the Queen's 'well-loved subjects'. Together with his cousin, Sir Francis Drake, he carried the hostilities against Spain right into their wealthy New World territories.

Spanish—even before he wiped out their great Armada in 1588—that they called him El Draque, the Dragon. He had a nose for treasure ships and was able to find them, almost instinctively, in the great expanses of ocean. The Spanish so feared this instinct that they believed he had a magic mirror which showed him where they hid.

After the treachery of San Juan de Ulloa, Drake sought revenge. He could not, however, operate officially as Elizabeth I was trying to forge Anglo-Spanish links and did not want to aggravate the situation by being seen to bless the actions of privateers. As he found that 'no recompense could be recovered out of Spain . . . by her Majesties letters' Drake carried out two voyages to the West Indies. These seem to have been in pursuit of legal trade. However, they were also undoubtedly reconnaissance missions.

By 1572, Drake had picked the target for his third voyage. This was the port of Nombre de Dios on the Caribbean coast of the Gulf of Darien (which lies between modern Colombia

The greatest seaman of his time, Drake was driven by hatred of Spanish treachery.

Below: Not all of Drake's exploits met with success. In 1558 he mounted an attack on Santiago in the Cape Verde Islands. He left empty-handed, as no treasure existed.

and Panama). This port was a treasure depot.

Drake's men stole into the harbour at night, and were split into two parties, one under his own command and the other under John Oxenham and Francis's brother, John Drake. They boldly marched into the town and took it unawares. In the half-light the citizens and garrison thought the raiders to be more numerous than they in fact were and fled, leaving the great silver and gold stores unguarded. Drake ordered his men to ignore the silver and capture the more valuable stocks of gold and gems. As they were trying to force the huge doors of the stronghouse, Drake fainted and was found to be suffering from a gunshot wound. Although Drake urged them to leave him and escape with the gold, they ignored him and carried him to the boats, leaving their booty.

Francis Drake lost his brother John during an assault on a frigate. By now Drake's force was reduced to 42, so he joined forces with some Maroons (or Cimarrons). These were black slaves who had escaped from the Spanish, lived in the jungle and hated their ex-masters. From them he learned of the bullion-laden mule trains that carried treasure down a highway through Panama. With 18 of his own men plus 30 Maroons, Drake set off on a hazardous overland route to ambush a mule train.

After a difficult journey, they reached a perfect spot for an attack. Drake organized an ambush, ordering his men to make no movement or noise. One, however, was a little drunk and allowed himself to be spotted by a passing horseman. Suspecting attack, the horseman rode forward to warn the approaching mule train. Pack animals loaded with cloth, food and small amounts of silver were quickly substituted for those with the gold. Therefore, when Drake's men fell upon them they found that the pickings were small.

Drake was now badly in need of plunder. His company was reduced to 31, and was not large enough to carry out attacks on well-guarded mule trains. Therefore, when he was sought out by a French privateer called Tetu with 70 men, he formed an alliance despite his deep mistrust of the man. He allowed only 20 of Tetu's men to join his own (thereby making sure that the French could not overwhelm him and make off with any spoil) and they set out in search of another bullion train. This venture met with greater success. Learning the lesson of stillness, the privateers kept well-hidden until a large train of 190 mules, carrying a total of nearly 30 tonnes of silver, came into view. The ambush was sprung and after a brief but

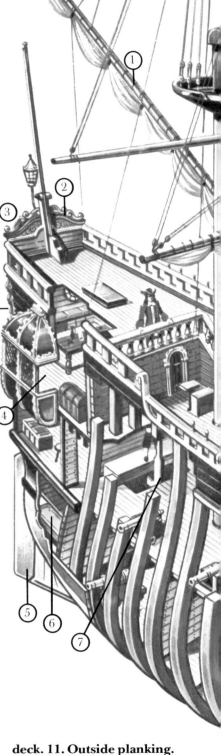

Right: Pirates not only plundered vessels but also took possession of suitable ships. This late 17th-century fighting ship is of the type a gang of pirates might endeavour to capture and use to further their thieving ways.

Key to the illustration:
1. Mizzenmast. 2. Stern carving. 3. Stern. 4. Captain's cabin. 5. Rudder. 6. Bunk room. 7. Rudder steering. 8. Sailmaker's and carpenter's room. 9. Lower gun deck. 10. Hatch and steps to lower deck. 11. Outside planking. 12. Gun port. 13. Galley. 14. Stem. 15. Figurehead. 16. Bowsprit. 17. Forestay. 18. Foresail. 19. Lifeboat. 20. Brass cannon. 21. Gun deck. 22. Quarter deck. 23. Mainstay. 24. Mizzenstay. 25. Mainsail.

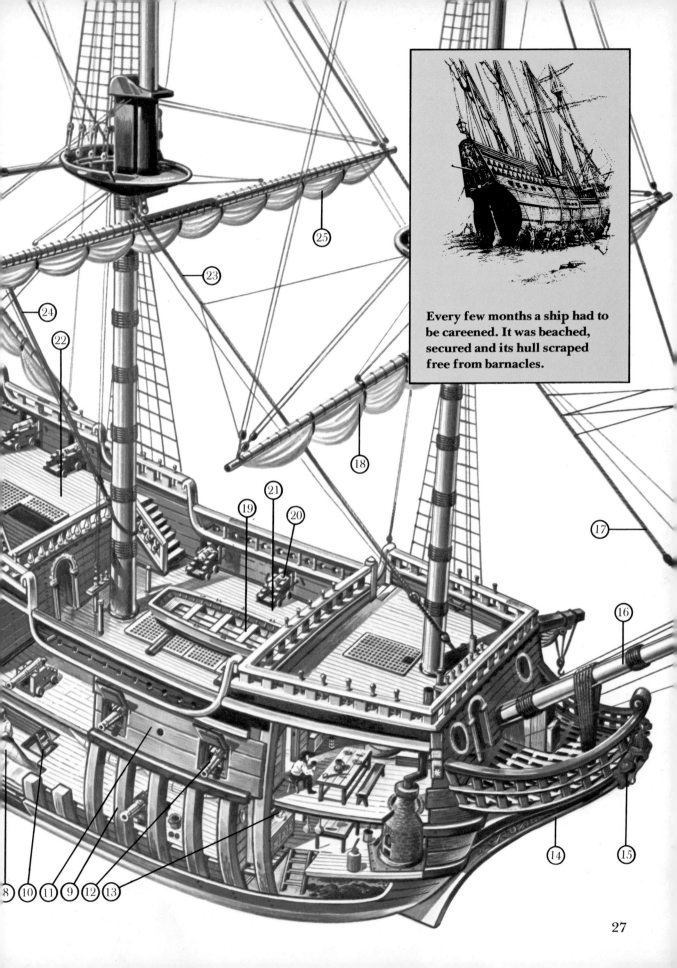

Every few months a ship had to
be careened. It was beached,
secured and its hull scraped
free from barnacles.

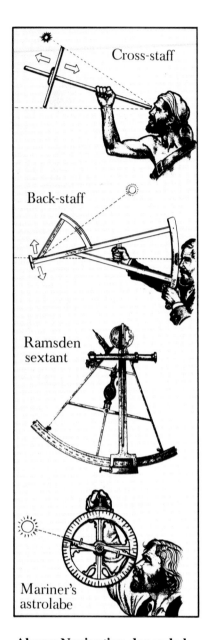

Cross-staff

Back-staff

Ramsden sextant

Mariner's astrolabe

Above: Navigation depended on plotting the ship's position in relation to the Sun or some other known astronomical point. The cross-staff was used to establish how far north or south the ship was by gauging the height of a fixed body. The back-staff measured the Sun's angle and altitude without dazzling the observer. The ramsden sextant established longitude and latitude. The mariner's astrolabe was originally developed by the ancient astronomers.

spirited skirmish the adventurers secured their prize.

There was far too much to be carried and Drake ordered that the bulkier bullion should be buried and collected at a later date. Loading themselves with what plunder they could carry, the privateers set off into the jungle. They left Tetu behind, as he had been wounded and also, unnoticed, a Frenchman who was too drunk to move. This man was easily caught by Spanish soldiers who tortured him until he revealed where the bullion was buried. The soldiers also found Tetu's hiding place and both prisoners were killed.

Nevertheless, Drake had gathered a great quantity of bullion and with this, and other prizes captured from the Spanish, he set sail for Plymouth where he arrived on Sunday, 9th August 1573 to a great welcome.

In spite of his privateering, Drake's fame resulted from his success as an explorer. He was the first Englishman to sail round the world. He did this between 1577 and 1580 some 58 years after Magellan, the Portuguese explorer, had made his first expedition. By finding a route round Cape Horn, Magellan had opened up the vast wealth of South America's Pacific coast and it was from the mines of Peru that Spain's gold and silver came.

During his great voyage of exploration, Drake, in the *Golden Hind*, battled through the Straits of Magellan and into the Pacific. There, he saw the chance of great profit and sailed up the coast of Chile towards Peru, where he hoped to find a treasure galleon sailing north to Panama. On 1st March 1579 they spotted the *Nuestra Señora de la Concepción*, nicknamed and better known as the *Cacafuego* or *Spitfire*. The Pacific was a Spanish ocean into which no English warship had ever ventured, and the treasure galleons plying it were lightly armed as they had nothing to fear. Any other ship spotted was assumed to be friendly and thus *Spitfire*'s captain, San Juan de Anton, showed no alarm when a tiny vessel approached him. This was his fatal mistake.

When the *Golden Hind* drew alongside, San Juan realized that she was English and that her master was the feared El Draque. A shot from Drake's cannon dismasted the *Spitfire* and the English sailors poured on board. There was little resistance from the Spanish sailors and before long San Juan and his ship were captured. What a prize she was! Perhaps the richest vessel Drake ever seized, crammed with gold, silver, and other gems thought to be worth, in modern terms, over ten million pounds!

The Spanish called Sir Francis Drake, El Draque which meant The Dragon, because of his fierce hounding of their ships. He was so expert at seeking them out in the vast tracts of ocean that they believed he had a magic mirror to show him their hiding places! Perhaps his greatest achievement was the capture of the *Nuestra Señora de la Concepción*, better known as the *Spitfire*. This was a daring stroke of bravado and entirely characteristic of the man who 'singed the King of Spain's beard' and routed the Armada.

One man who fell foul of the law's blurred distinction between piracy and privateering was Captain William Kidd. It is difficult to tell from the evidence that remains, whether Kidd was a villainous, black-hearted pirate, or an honest, but foolish, privateer betrayed by his patrons. Certainly, Kidd gained his early reputation as a bold and gallant privateer who had served his country well by attacking French shipping during the war of 1689. Six years later, the English merchant shipping threat came from pirates who operated in the Indian Ocean from bases in Madagascar. The navy could not be spared to fight them and so Kidd was selected and, it appears, secretly commissioned to seek and destroy any pirate vessels. The authority behind this seems to have been Lord Belmont, the governor of New York. Like the rest of America's northern seaboard states, New York was then a colony of England. To confuse the situation, Kidd also carried Letters of Marque from William III of England enabling him to attack French shipping.

Kidd set out in 1695 and for a year met with little success. His crew were restless, provisions were low and their pockets empty. Mutiny was in the air. On 30th October 1697 a confrontation took place on deck. Kidd was either attacked—or imagined he was being attacked—by gunner William Moore; he retaliated by striking the man across the head with a heavy bucket. As a result of the blow, Moore died. It would appear that Kidd, desperate and fearful of mutiny, then turned to piracy and exceeded his licence as a privateer. Certainly stories abound of his cruel behaviour, and the torture and murder of innocent people aboard ships and in island villages throughout the Indian Ocean, but these have not been proved.

In January 1698, Kidd captured a large and valuable ship, the *Quedagh Merchant*. Although Armenian in origin, it appears that she was sailing under the flag of protection of the French and, therefore, within Kidd's brief as a privateer. He also captured another Armenian ship, the *Maiden* and from both ships took, and carefully kept, passes guaranteeing protection for the ships from the French government.

After sailing into the pirate stronghold of Madagascar, where most of his crew deserted, Kidd set course back to England and, on the way learnt that he had been declared a pirate and was wanted for the murder of William Moore. Certain that he was innocent of the charges he contacted his

Ram
Sponge
Bristle
Powder ladle
Worm (charge-remover)

1

2

3

4

patron, Lord Belmont, and entrusted him with the passes captured from the *Quedagh Merchant* and the *Maiden.* He was reassured by Belmont's reply: 'I make no manner of doubt but to obtain the King's pardon for you.'

However, the Governor was playing a devious game. He was told to seize Kidd and was obviously eager to cover up the fact that he had secretly employed the Captain as a privateer. Kidd was arrested and sent under guard to London where he spent 13 months in Newgate Prison awaiting trial.

From the beginning it was obvious that Kidd had been deserted by his powerful backers and left to fend for himself. He was allowed no counsel and had to defend himself against six charges, the three main ones being of piratical attack

Carrack (35 metres)

Dutch merchant ship (28 metres)

William Dampier was one of the most cultured and intelligent privateers of his time. He travelled the world and wrote of his adventures. He helped rescue Alexander Selkirk, who was the model for Daniel Defoe's book, *Robinson Crusoe*.

English great ship (56 metres)

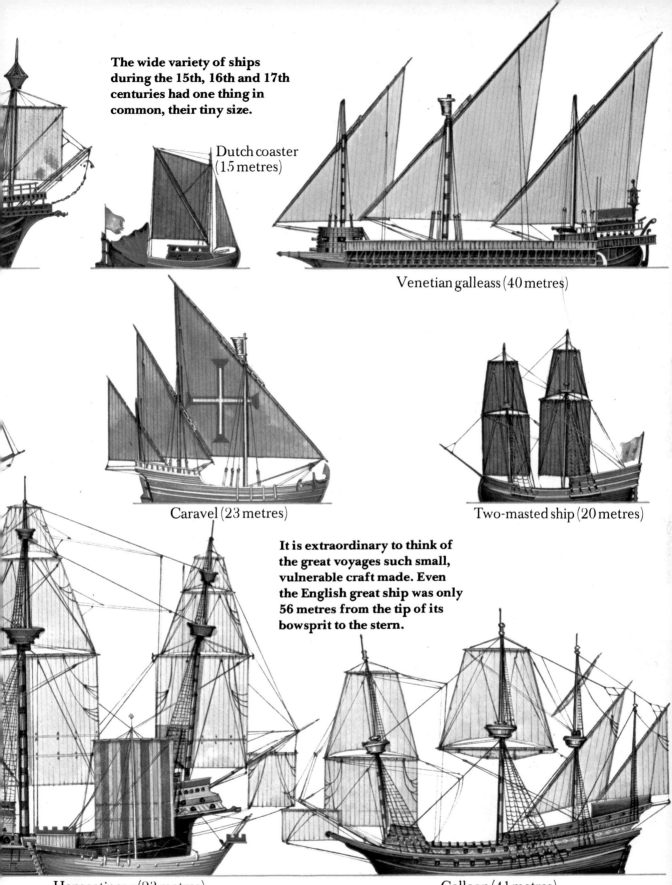

The wide variety of ships during the 15th, 16th and 17th centuries had one thing in common, their tiny size.

Dutch coaster (15 metres)

Venetian galleass (40 metres)

Caravel (23 metres)

Two-masted ship (20 metres)

It is extraordinary to think of the great voyages such small, vulnerable craft made. Even the English great ship was only 56 metres from the tip of its bowsprit to the stern.

Hanseatic cog (23 metres)

Galleon (41 metres)

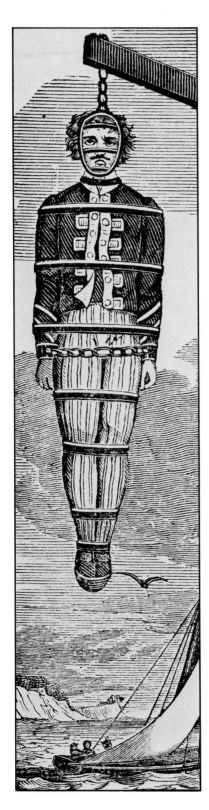

The unfortunate Captain Kidd's body was hoisted in chains and hoops after his execution and publicly displayed as a grim warning.

upon the two Armenian vessels and the murder of Moore. His defence rested on the fact that the two passes proved the ships to have been French and therefore fair game, and that he had struck Moore—a mutineer—in self-defence.

The passes had mysteriously disappeared (and were not to be discovered for 200 years) and the evidence against him came from witnesses who turned king's evidence in order to escape being executed for piracy. Against such odds Kidd was powerless. He was found guilty, hanged and his body displayed in chains as a gruesome warning to others tempted to become pirates.

Henry Morgan was, without question, a brutal buccaneer (a pirate of the Caribbean) but his murderous, if daring, activities had a dubious stamp of approval. Oliver Cromwell, England's Lord Protector, had requested permission to trade in the Spanish Caribbean but was refused. He decided, therefore, to capture some Spanish possessions and force the issue. Subsequently Jamaica was taken and became English territory; in retaliation Spain declared war and English governors of Jamaica started issuing Letters of Marque to any brigand who would carry on the 'war' by raiding Spanish treasure galleons. In this way, cut-throat mariners were given the rather insubstantial shelter of English law for as long as the war lasted. As long as they confined their attack to Spanish ships and towns, they were safe from prosecution.

This arrangement allowed Morgan to prosper, although at any other time he would have been hunted down as a pirate. His first notable achievement as a buccaneer chief was to march on Santa Maria de Puerto Principe (now Camaguey in Cuba). His highly-disciplined crew fought off attacks from men on horseback and entered the town where they starved and tortured the inhabitants until they revealed the whereabouts of their stores of treasure.

In 1668, Morgan led a raid on the important treasure harbour of Porto Bello in Panama which was defended by three castles. The first castle was captured after a fight but the inhabitants of the second resisted stoutly. Morgan herded together priests and nuns and drove them forward, convinced that the defenders would not risk killing their clergy. The Spaniards did fire, however, and finally gave in only after the bloodiest of battles. The third castle surrendered immediately. The treasure stored in the town's strongroom, plus huge sums raised through ransom, gave Morgan a massive booty and a reputation as the most successful buccaneer in the Caribbean.

Morgan continued his raids on Spanish towns. He plundered Maracaibo (in modern Venezuela) and got money by using his usual brutish torture. One of his favoured methods of extracting information was the use of a makeshift rack. He would break both his victim's arms, then tie thongs round his wrists and ankles and secure them to stakes driven into the ground. The unfortunate man would be bearing his whole weight on them; as if this was not cruel enough, Morgan would then place huge rocks on the man's

Two aspects of the life of the notorious, but colourful, Henry Morgan. Above: An illustration showing the more bawdy side of his nature. Below: Morgan's crude, barbarous rack. Rocks were piled on the victim's body until he revealed his secrets.

stomach, gradually increasing the load and greatly increasing the agony.

Despite his atrocities, Morgan received the patronage and encouragement of the governor of Jamaica as he had a financial interest in some of Morgan's expeditions. He was mildly rebuked by the governor for his excesses and then commissioned to make his biggest raid of all. He assembled a mighty fleet of 36 ships, carrying 2,000 men in addition to the vessels' crews, and set out for Panama which was thought to be the richest city of the Central American mainland.

On the way to Panama City, Morgan attacked and captured fortresses on Santa Catalina Island. He also took Chagres in Panama after a furious battle and then continued overland towards his main target. On the way his force suffered greatly through illness, insufficient food and Indian attacks which reduced their numbers alarmingly. Eventually they reached their goal only to find that the Spaniards were warned and ready. Outside the walls of the city troops of cavalry were waiting. Also, a herd of wild bulls were stampeded forward with the intention of breaking the pirates' ranks. However, the sound of battle turned the bulls who tore through the Spanish ranks instead. The cavalry charged across marshy ground,

Above: Everyday life on board a pirate vessel was largely uneventful. When not engaged on expeditions of pillage and plunder the pirates would indulge in gambling and drinking to relieve the boredom. The more industrious crew members might polish their weapons for the next battle, or try to clean their filthy quarters, some simply slept. Left: The natural haunts of pirates and privateers were in groups of islands and indented coasts where they could anchor safely without fear of discovery. This painting shows privateers of the 17th century sheltering in the old port of La Rochelle in France.

became bogged down and the riders offered easy targets for Morgan's sharp-shooters.

The Spanish defenders inside the walls lost courage when they saw their main line of defence had been broken and fought on only half-heartedly. Soon Panama fell to Morgan and his men. The booty was huge and when it had been collected together, the once-proud city was put to the torch and totally destroyed.

Although Morgan's treatment of prisoners was extremely cruel there was no doubting his qualities of leadership and military skill. The sacking of Panama was his greatest achievement and, on his return to Jamaica, the governing council passed a vote of thanks even though England and Spain had signed a treaty ending the war. The end of the war unfortunately made Morgan a pirate rather than a privateer. The Spanish government's protests to Charles II of England were so loud that Morgan was shipped to England to stand trial. However, public opinion hailed Morgan as a hero, his atrocities were glossed over and instead of bringing him to trial, Charles knighted him. As a final irony, he was appointed deputy governor of Jamaica and given the job of suppressing buccaneers!

Buccaneers of the Caribbean

As we have already discovered, the pirates who infested the Caribbean and the American coast were known as buccaneers. This came from the French word *boucan*, a simple form of barbecue over which strips of meat were smoked. The original *boucaniers* (later buccaneers) hunted wild cattle that roamed on the islands of the Caribbean. Later these rough men started plundering settlements and used small boats to prey on light trading vessels. This gradually developed into full-scale piracy with large, well-armed ships.

The targets of the buccaneers were, of course, the bullion ships carrying the wealth of the New World to Spain and the colonies, and stores of treasure that lined the Central and Southern American coastline. The prospect of such rich plunder attracted criminals, army deserters, adventurers and even gentlemen. Others included experienced seamen who had either been laid off from established navies at the end of a war or those who could no longer stand the foul conditions, harsh discipline and poor pay of the merchant service.

To a sailor, the risk of death in battle or at the end of a rope, was compensated for by the advantages of a pirate's life. In pirate vessels a rough democracy (unknown in traditional, legal ships) operated. The crew voted the ablest and often the luckiest (as good luck in a leader was very necessary among superstitious seamen) man to be captain and followed him as long as he was successful. Failure usually meant that a captain was deposed and replaced by a better man. This freedom of choice often extended to the choice of targets, each man voting on whether the risks involved were worth the prize. Discipline was generally lax with no floggings for minor offences such as was found in conventional fleets. Alcohol was frequently available and riotous drinking marked the long days when no prey appeared on the horizon.

Most buccaneers operated under a set of rules known as Pirates' Articles. These laid down how a prize was to be shared. Booty was allotted in proportion to seniority (again, each of the officers was elected according to ability); the most senior officer was the captain (who had supreme control only when in battle) and those who controlled the ship's day-to-day running such as the quartermaster, who had greatest executive power, sailing master, gunner, boson and watch-keeping officers. In addition there was a crude insurance policy that awarded compensation to the dependents of men

Once started, a battle between pirates and their victims could go on for hours and often continued as darkness fell. Pirates would use special equipment to capture a vessel. Top inset: two types of cannon shot: 1. Designed to tear sails and rigging.
2. Anti-personnel shot. Bottom inset: grappling hook.

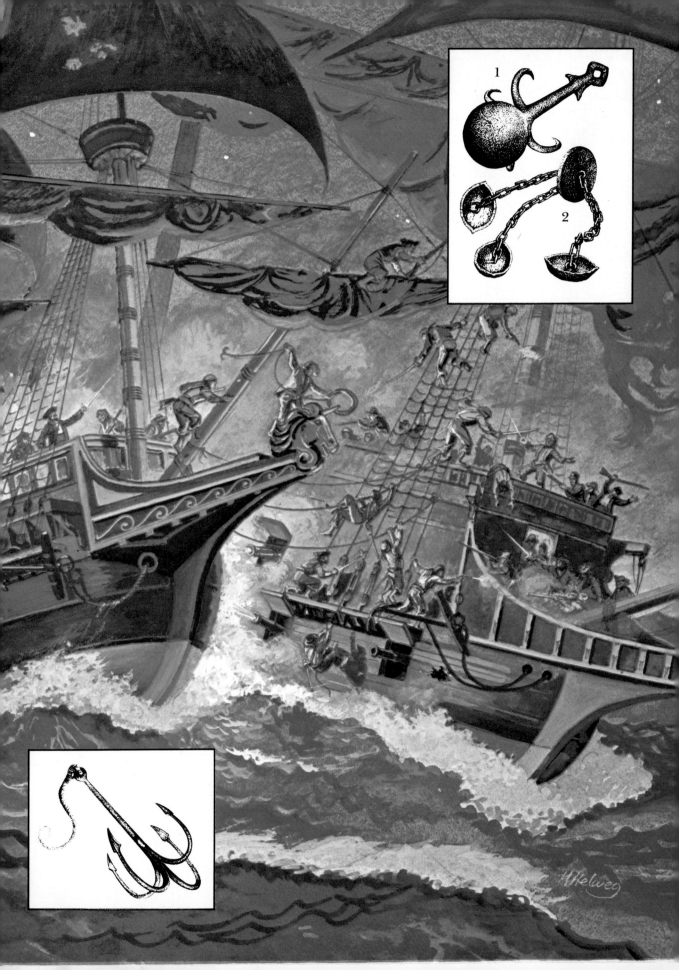

Above: Captain Bartholomew Roberts composed the Pirates' Charter and favoured a short, merry life!

killed in action, as well as to those who met with serious injuries, such as the loss of a limb or an eye.

The quartermaster was responsible for discipline. He could order floggings and even marooning. This meant leaving a man on some lonely shore with only basic food supplies, tools and weapons. The intention was that he could survive until picked up by a passing vessel but would not be able to give accurate information as to the pirates' whereabouts as the interval would be too great for him. 'Walking the plank' seems to be the invention of popular fiction.

Although there were always men willing to become outlaws, it is unlikely that they volunteered in sufficient numbers to support the great number of pirate ships that operated in the Caribbean. There was a pirates' equivalent of the press-gang used by navies to recruit men, particularly skilled officers like surgeons, navigators and gunners. When a ship was taken, expert crew members were frequently urged to sign the Pirates' Articles and become pirates. Many took to the life and remained buccaneers.

Passengers captured during an action were treated with brutality or courtesy, depending on the captain and the discipline he exercised over his crew. Wealthy and influential prisoners were usually given great hospitality while awaiting the payment of ransom. Lesser mortals could expect rough treatment and some suffered greatly. In general, pirates were rough, cruel men, sparing little sympathy for those unfortunate enough to fall into their hands. There was the occasional display of decency, but only very rarely.

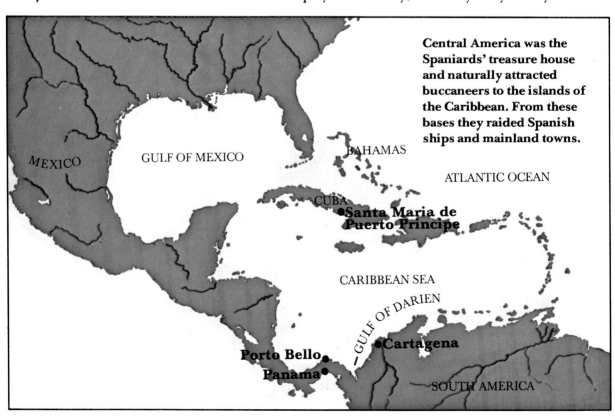

Central America was the Spaniards' treasure house and naturally attracted buccaneers to the islands of the Caribbean. From these bases they raided Spanish ships and mainland towns.

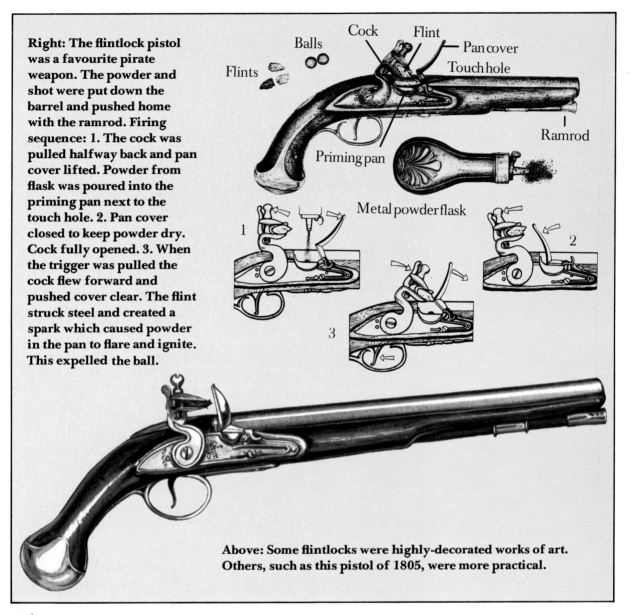

Right: The flintlock pistol was a favourite pirate weapon. The powder and shot were put down the barrel and pushed home with the ramrod. Firing sequence: 1. The cock was pulled halfway back and pan cover lifted. Powder from flask was poured into the priming pan next to the touch hole. 2. Pan cover closed to keep powder dry. Cock fully opened. 3. When the trigger was pulled the cock flew forward and pushed cover clear. The flint struck steel and created a spark which caused powder in the pan to flare and ignite. This expelled the ball.

Flints Balls Cock Flint Pan cover Touch hole

Ramrod

Priming pan Metal powder flask

1 2 3

Above: Some flintlocks were highly-decorated works of art. Others, such as this pistol of 1805, were more practical.

Isolated coves, like this one in St Lucia, sheltered pirates.

Captured crew members who were not useful as forced men, could expect little mercy. Many were undoubtedly slaughtered, some simply thrown overboard. Others were cast adrift in small boats with little hope of survival. The captured vessels were treated according to their usefulness. A swift, well-armed ship would be commandeered as the pirate chief's flagship (rivals vied with each other for the handsomest craft); other good boats would be added to the buccaneers' fleet if they had men enough to crew them. Those considered worthless or too badly damaged were scuppered or burnt after they had been stripped of stores and tackle.

Buccaneers were generally French or English. At first their attacks were limited to Spanish ships and towns. However, after the Treaty of Utrecht in 1713 the English government frowned on buccaneering and determined to bring the newly-declared pirates to heel. Naval operations were, on the whole, unsuccessful and so an amnesty was announced. Any pirate who surrendered was promised the King's pardon. Some were offered farm land but proved untrustworthy, and neglected their properties and soon drifted back into piracy.

There were intermittent and mostly futile naval sweeps against buccaneers during the 18th century. In the early 19th century the Americans, together with the Spanish and the British Royal Navy, attacked the problem in earnest. The West Indies were the worst affected areas because they were rich in trade. In the campaign of 1823-4 about 1,300 pirates were caught or killed. The tide had turned; continual pressure was applied and by the 1850s piracy in the Caribbean was virtually over.

In the heyday of buccaneering there were many colourful and daring pirates whose names we still know. The traditional image of the freebooting, swashbuckling pirate comes from such great buccaneers as Blackbeard and Bartholomew Roberts who sailed under the flag of the grinning skull and crossbones—the dreaded Jolly Roger.

Perhaps the most notorious pirate of them all was Blackbeard. So many myths surround this man and so few accredited facts have been established, that he appears to be a figure of fiction rather than fact. Nonetheless, he *did* exist.

His name was Edward Teach and he was thought to have been born in either Bristol or Jamaica. The exact year of his birth is not known nor is his career before piracy. Some people claim that he served as a privateer against the French during the war of 1702-13. In any event, by 1716 he had started on his brief but notorious career as a pirate.

Blackbeard is remembered mainly for two extraordinary pieces of showmanship. The first was his amazing appearance. His nickname arose from his long, matted and filthy beard. So extensive was it that it appeared to merge with his long, straggly hair. To emphasize its effect and to appear even more ferocious, he plaited long, slow-burning matches (similar to the touch-fuses used by gunners to light the firing-powder of their cannon) into it and set them ablaze. As he leapt into the attack, with his hair appearing to be on fire, a cutlass in each hand and six pistols slung round his chest, he must have appeared to be the Devil himself.

The second incredible 'fact' was his boast that he had taken 14 wives. It is impossible to know if this was true, but some authorities claim that Blackbeard would carry off a woman of his fancy, take her aboard his ship and have a member of his crew perform a mock 'marriage service'. Other tales suggest that he forced his 'wives' to dance for his entertainment by firing his pistols at their feet.

Such tales, whether true or false, certainly caused fear and loathing on the part of the people of the American seaboard, who were the primary objects of Blackbeard's attacks. In view of the rumours that anyone who resisted having their rings stolen would have their fingers hacked off as well, it is no wonder that Blackbeard was considered the most dangerous brigand of his time.

Above: No pirate ever had a worse reputation than Edward Teach, the despicable Blackbeard. He relished his notoriety and made his appearance as loathsome as possible. The 18th-century engraving (inset) shows the slow-burning matches he plaited into his hair. He treated both crew and victims with utmost savagery. The Jolly Roger was the pirates' standard and was often personalized. The top flag was flown by Calico Jack Rackham, the bottom one by Black Barty.

Blackbeard cruised the waters off America in his flagship *Queen Anne's Revenge*, preying on shipping and shore bases and occasionally skirmishing with Royal Navy ships. He blockaded the port of Charleston, South Carolina for several days, holding some captured sailors to ransom. They were eventually exchanged for a medicine chest worth a mere £350. This made people wonder whether Blackbeard was perhaps a drug addict or suffered from disease. Blackbeard's rampages continued for two years, during which time the governor of North Carolina joined him as a partner in his enterprise. Eventually his behaviour became so outrageous that a deputation was sent to the governor of Virginia imploring him to despatch a naval craft to stop the villain.

In reply, Lieutenant Maynard and H.M.S. *Pearl* together with H.M.S. *Lime*, were given the job of hunting down Blackbeard. They ran him to ground one evening at Ocracoke Inlet in Pamlico Sound, North Carolina. Maynard decided to delay the attack until the next day. The night before the battle Blackbeard spent the time in drunken revelry with his henchman. At one point, he pulled out two pistols and fired them under the table. As a result his sailing-master, Israel Hands (immortalized in Robert Louis Stevenson's *Treasure Island*), was shot in the knee and permanently lamed.

As dawn rose Maynard ordered his two sloops to move in and the battle commenced. The water was so shallow that manoeuvrability was severely restricted, and after fierce exchanges Maynard's vessel began drifting towards Blackbeard's. Hoping to tempt the pirate into boarding his sloop, Maynard ordered all his men into the hold where they were to wait, ready to spring out in a surprise attack.

Blackbeard fell for the ruse. He leapt aboard with 14 men, only to be met by Maynard's determined crew. The hand-to-hand fighting was fierce but the pirates were steadily overwhelmed until Blackbeard alone remained alive. He battled like a mad bull and despite bullet wounds and a score of sword slashes kept up the struggle. Eventually he fell—some say by a pistol shot from Maynard, others by two massive cuts across the neck from a cutlass—and died on the deck. Maynard had the massive shaggy head cut from the body and attached to his boat as a trophy.

Another interesting character was Captain Bartholomew Roberts, known also as 'Black Barty'. During his career he sailed the Caribbean, along the American coast as far north as Newfoundland, and through West African waters in search of plunder. His skill and daring was rewarded with the capture of more than 400 ships.

He was unusual in that he appeared to be a man of high moral standards. He did not drink and forbade his men to gamble; he ordered all lights aboard to be put out by eight o'clock each night. This, in fact, was a sensible precaution because many a ship was lost when lanterns were knocked over in drunken high spirits or brawls. He instituted a Pirates' Charter that laid down conditions of service and a disciplinary code. In short, he ran, by pirate standards, a tight ship and this undoubtedly helped towards his success.

Roberts started, like so many of his kind, as an honest seaman. He worked hard and had reached the position of second mate on a slave ship when it was taken by pirates. Roberts was unwilling to join the pirate crew but was forced to because of his navigational skill. His resistance did not last long and later he was to declare that a 'merry life and a short one' would be his motto.

Roberts' abilities quickly became clear to his fellows and he was elected leader. He started his career as a pirate captain with a sensational coup. By boldly sailing in among a fleet of Portuguese treasure ships loaded with bullion from Brazil, he managed to take one from under the escort's nose. With this success to spur him on he roamed the seas searching for fresh victims. Ship after ship fell to him, many without a fight. The sight of his huge pirate flag seemed to frighten most of them into instant submission. This may seem extraordinary but it

should be remembered that many crews were unwilling to risk their lives to save the property of ship-owners who so frequently treated them badly.

Roberts became such a menace in the Caribbean that the governors of Barbados and Martinique made determined, if futile, efforts to stop him. Roberts took unkindly to this and had a Jolly Roger, a pirate flag, made that showed him, cutlass in hand, standing on a pair of skulls. Under one were the letters A.B.H. (for A Barbadian's Head) and under the other, A.M.H. (A Martiniquian's Head). This appealed to his vanity which also found expression in the clothes he wore. He dressed like a gentleman and before any action put on silk stockings, damask breeches and coat and set a fine red feather in his hat.

The governors of Martinique and Barbados were not fated to catch the wily Roberts. He sailed out of Caribbean waters and across the South Atlantic to prey on the shipping of West Africa. Here his seamanship and boldness were well-rewarded until the relatively easy pickings made him careless. In February, 1721 H.M.S. *Swallow*, which had been ordered to seek out and take Roberts, spotted his sail off Cape Lopez (now in Gabon). Roberts was at breakfast and his crew were suffering sorely after a night of heavy drinking.

Swallow sailed in close and fired a great broadside of cannon and small arms. Almost immediately Roberts was hit in the throat and died soon afterwards. His crew, seeing further resistance was useless, surrendered and consigned their captain's body, dressed in all its finery, to the sea. He died in the manner he had wished and was saved from the fate which befell 52 members of his crew, who were hanged. His life had indeed been short and merry.

One of the clauses of the Pirates' Charter stated that 'No boy or woman is to be allowed on board.' The penalty for disregarding this clause was death. Considering the dangers and hardships of life on board a pirate ship, it is hard to imagine why any women would have been attracted to such a life, but in fact several were.

Anne Bonny was the daughter of an Irish lawyer, but spent her childhood in Charleston, South Carolina. She was an independent and high spirited young girl, and at 16 eloped with a seaman named James Bonny. James signed on with a pirate crew, and only a short time after their marriage, Anne fell in love with another pirate called Calico Jack Rackham. She managed to persuade Rackham to let her accompany him on his sea voyages by disguising herself as a seaman.

During one of these voyages, Rackham captured a Dutch merchantman and forced the only English sailor to join his pirate crew. By this time, Anne had also tired of Calico Jack and turned her attention to the new crewman, Mark Reid. She was, however, astonished to discover that 'he' was in fact a woman, and her name was Mary Read. Mary's history was

Anne Bonny cuts a dashing figure in this 18th-century print, dressed in men's clothes and armed with pistol, sword and axe.

45

more extraordinary than Anne's, as she had actually been brought up as a boy and spent some time in the Royal Navy. Hating the brutality of naval life, Mary deserted in Flanders, and then enlisted as a foot soldier. Keeping her disguise as a man, Mary remained a loyal and gallant soldier until she fell in love with a young corporal. She revealed her true identity to him and they left the army to become landlords of a tavern. However, her husband was killed and Mary decided to return to sea and eventually found herself among Rackham's pirate crew, once more disguised as a man.

Thus, by a strange coincidence Rackham sailed with two fierce female pirates. The indomitable pair soon became well known, and could always be relied upon to put up as good a fight as their male counterparts. They enjoyed several years of successful piracy before Rackham's ship was eventually cornered by a naval sloop. Rackham was not a very capable captain and had little heart for a fight. He and most of his men hid in the hold whilst Mary Read and Anne Bonny greeted the boarding party with a spirited fight. However, they were soon overcome and the whole crew was captured. All were tried for piracy and found guilty. Rackham was hanged, but the two women escaped the gallows. Shortly after Mary died in prison of fever, but Anne lived on quietly for many more years.

Not all the Caribbean buccaneers were British or of British descent. One of the most infamous was a Frenchman named Jean François Nau, known throughout the Caribbean as L'Olonnois after the village of his birth, or simply 'The Torturer'.

Above: L'Olonnois, whose brutality challenged Blackbeard's.
Below: Mary Read was an expert with small arms. Once, a bully challenged her lover to a duel. Mary picked a fight with his opponent and demanded instant satisfaction. After a fierce fight with pistol and cutlass, Mary triumphed and her lover lived.

Many tales are told of his brutality. When he attacked the town of Maracaibo, (a favourite pirate target which is now in Venezuela) it is said that he walked along a line of prisoners decapitating each in turn and licking the blood from his sword. During a raid on another town, L'Olonnois needed to be guided along a safe path in order to avoid an ambush. When the prisoners were unwilling to help it is said he took one, slashed open his body and ripped out his heart. This he proceeded to eat before the astonished and revolted captives who quickly consented to his will.

Raids on other Spanish towns were accompanied by such atrocities. But, if the stories are to be believed, this monster met with a fitting end. After a storm wrecked his ship he was washed up on a wild shore. There he was found by Indians who dismembered his living body and threw the torn limbs on to a fire.

Hollywood films have undoubtedly romanticized the characters and exploits of the pirates who sailed the Spanish Main. That great cinema swashbuckler, Errol Flynn, specialized in playing a seagoing version of Robin Hood and, although greatly exaggerated, there is a basis of truth in the characterization. The model might be a Frenchman called Ravenaux De Luson. He was born a gentleman and inherited a substantial sum which he squandered by gambling. Like several before him he sought a life of adventure and saw buccaneering as a pleasant and comparatively easy way to restore his fortune. He was deeply religious and prevented his men from sacking churches or harming any member of the clergy. He was gallant and courteous to women and showed great hospitality towards his captives.

His exploits in the Caribbean and among the treasure ships of the Pacific earned him a considerable fortune which he managed to keep. He eventually retired from piracy and returned to take what he considered his rightful place in French society and wrote an account of his adventures.

However, colourful and romantic though they might sometimes appear, pirates were actually nothing more than common criminals. They caused great suffering, misery and loss to innocent passengers, sailors and merchants; they murdered, tortured and robbed; they flaunted the law and international convention. They were a blight that had to be purged from the sea-lanes before trade could flourish. It was not until the end of the 19th century, however, that piracy was removed from the oceans. Indeed, it was not until 1856 that privateering was officially abolished by international consent with the Declaration of Paris; with a degree of political stability in Europe, these 'official' pirates were not needed.

Today piracy is mostly unknown. Nothing remains of the pirates, corsairs, buccaneers and privateers except a glossy, glamorized memory of sails, fluttering black flags, booming cannon and lithe, muscular, smiling villains swinging on ropes, with cutlasses clenched between their teeth. In piracy, as in so many other things, fiction is far more attractive than the true facts.

Above: As outlaws of the sea pirates knew that they could expect no mercy if they were caught. Their punishments were as hard and as cruel as the brutalities the pirates themselves inflicted on their victims.

Glossary

ARMADA Spanish fleet defeated by the English in 1588.

BARBARY COAST The coast of North Africa.

BEY Turkish governor of district or province.

BOOTY Treasure or goods seized in an attack or raid.

BOSON Officer in charge of the sails and rigging who calls the men to their duties with a whistle (short for Boatswain).

BOWSPRIT Small mast projecting over a ship's bow (pronounced bo-sprit).

BRIGANTINE Two-masted merchant ship.

BUCCANEER A Portuguese, English, Dutch or French pirate of the Caribbean opposing Spain in the 17th century.

BULLION Gold and silver, usually coins.

CANNON Muzzle-loaded gun mounted on board ship.

CARIBBEAN Part of the Atlantic Ocean between the West Indies and the shores of Central and South America.

CLIPPER An extremely fast three-masted sailing ship developed for trade in 1845.

COFFER Strong-box used for storing valuables.

CORSAIR Pirate of the Mediterranean and North African coast. Derived from the French *corsaire*, meaning one who courses or ranges.

EMIR Saracen or Arab governor.

FLAGSHIP Ship carrying an admiral or other fleet commander.

FLOTILLA Fleet of small boats.

FORAY A raid.

FORECASTLE Forward section of a ship, often containing the crew's quarters (pronounced foke-sel).

GALLEON Large ship, high in stem and stern. Used to carry heavy cargo. It was the classic Spanish treasure ship.

GALLIOT Light ship favoured by the corsairs. Powered by oars and sails.

GARRISON A place where soldiers are stationed.

HALBERD A weapon with an axe-head on one side and a sharp spike on the other. Mounted on a long staff.

HATCH Cover to opening on ship's deck.

HOLD The large area below deck where cargo or booty is stored.

JUNK Flat-bottomed Chinese sailing boat with a square prow and a very prominent stern.

LETTER OF MARQUE The official commission given to a privateer, usually by his monarch. It gave him permission to attack and rob enemy shipping.

MANDARIN An important Chinese official.

MARINES Soldiers serving in a navy.

MERCHANTMAN Large trading ship.

MOSLEMS People who follow the teachings of Mohammed through the Islamic religion.

MUSKET An early hand-held infantry gun.

MUTINY To rebel against the captain and officers of a ship.

PERAHU Malaysian oar-powered boat. It could be very large, carrying 100 oarsmen and up to 150 warriors.

PLUNDER To rob or steal. Often used to describe the stolen goods themselves.

PRIVATEER A captain licensed by Letter of Marque. It was also the term used to describe his ship.

RANSACK Search thoroughly.

SCIMITAR A short, curved, single-edged sword, used mostly by Turks and Persians.

SCUPPER To sink a ship.

SKIRMISH A disorganized attack or petty fight between two, usually small, bodies of men.

SLOOP A one-masted light vessel. Naval or war sloops, however, might have had more than one mast and carried between ten and eighteen guns.

SPOILS OF WAR The possessions, treasure, money, etc. taken from the loser of a brief fight, or battle, by the winner.

SQUADRON A division of ships.

XEBEC A three-masted sailing ship that was used by corsairs.